Wild About Wheels

# Race Cars

by Mari Schuh

PEBBLE
a capstone imprint

Pebble Emerge is published by Pebble, an imprint of Capstone.
1710 Roe Crest Drive
North Mankato, Minnesota 56003
www.capstonepub.com

**Library of Congress Cataloging-in-Publication Data is available on the Library
of Congress website.**
ISBN: 978-1-9771-2483-8 (hardcover)
ISBN: 978-1-9771-2525-5 (eBook PDF)

Summary: Describes race cars, including the different kinds of race cars, their
features, and how they reach such amazing speeds.

**Image Credits**
Associated Press: Reinhold Matay, 10; Capstone Studio: Karon Dubke, 21;
Dreamstime: Walter Arce, 9; Newscom: Cal Sport Media/Russell Hons, 4, Icon SMI/
David Allio, 15; Shutterstock: action sports, 6, 14, Action Sports Photography, 5, 7,
18, Admad Faizal Yahya, 13, HodagMedia, 16, Jens Mommens, cover, back cover,
John J. Klaiber Jr, 12, Mladen Pavlovic, 8, Natursports, 17, 19, Phillip Rubino, 11,
StevanZZ, background (race track)

**Editorial Credits**
Editor: Carrie Sheely; Designer: Cynthia Della-Rovere;
Media Researcher: Eric Gohl; Production Specialist: Katy LaVigne

All internet sites appearing in back matter were available and accurate when this
book was sent to press.

Printed and bound in the USA.
003422

# Table of Contents

What Race Cars Do . . . . . . . . . . . 4

Look Inside. . . . . . . . . . . . . . . . . . 8

Look Outside. . . . . . . . . . . . . . . . 12


Race Car Diagrams . . . . . . . . 18

Design Your Own Race Car . . 20

Glossary . . . . . . . . . . . . . . . . . . 22

Read More . . . . . . . . . . . . . . . . 23

Internet Sites . . . . . . . . . . . . . . 23

Index . . . . . . . . . . . . . . . . . . . . 24

Words in **bold** are in the glossary.

# What Race Cars Do

Vroom! Race cars zoom around the track. They come around the curve and zip toward the finish line. Which one will win?

Race cars are built for speed. Some cars race on **paved** tracks. Other cars race on dirt tracks. But they all are very fast!

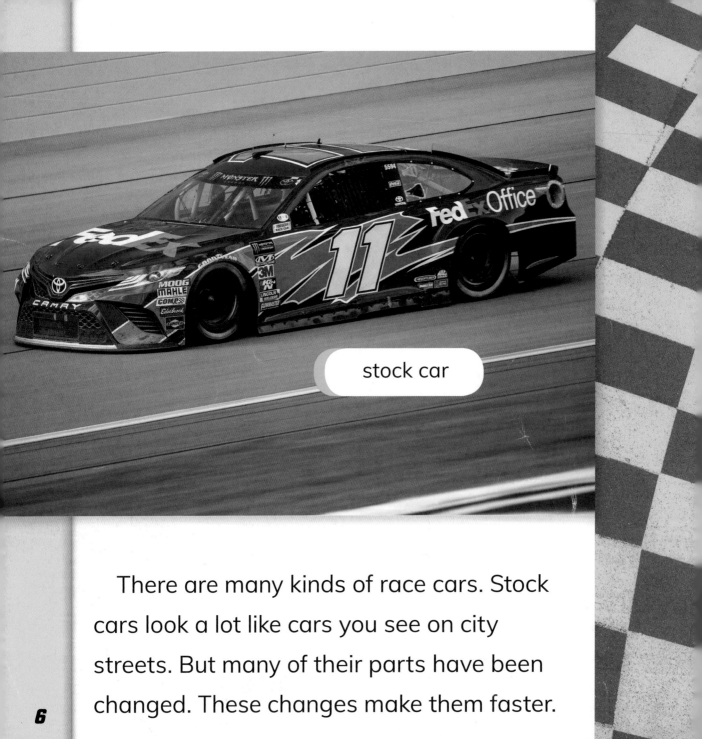

stock car

There are many kinds of race cars. Stock cars look a lot like cars you see on city streets. But many of their parts have been changed. These changes make them faster.

Some race cars have open wheels. That means the wheels are not covered. The **cockpit** is open too. The driver's head sticks out. IndyCars and Formula 1 (F1) cars are open-wheel cars.

IndyCar

# LOOK INSIDE

Look inside the cockpit! A harness keeps the driver in place. The driver turns the car with the steering wheel. It often has many switches, knobs, and dials. Some change the way the car balances in corners. Others send messages to the driver's crew.

F1 car steering wheel

harness

stock car engine

Race cars have big **engines**. The engines can be in the car's front or back. They give race cars power to reach high speeds. Top fuel **dragsters** can go more than 300 miles (483 kilometers) per hour!

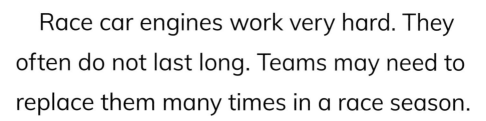

Race car engines work very hard. They often do not last long. Teams may need to replace them many times in a race season.

top fuel dragster

# LOOK OUTSIDE

Normal car tires have bumps or **grooves** called tread. Cars that race on dirt tracks do too.

tire with tread

Many tires for paved tracks are smooth. They are called slicks. During a race, the tires get hot. They get sticky. They grip the dry track. Slicks wear out quickly. Many tires are used in one race.

slick

Race cars are colorful. They are covered in stickers called **decals**. Many cars have fancy paint jobs. They often have a big number on the sides. This helps fans watching the race. It's easier to see each car as it speeds around the track.

Race cars have lots of parts to help drivers. Many race cars have **wings** or **spoilers**. These parts help push air down. This helps the tires grip the track. The car can go faster while turning.

rear wing

front wing

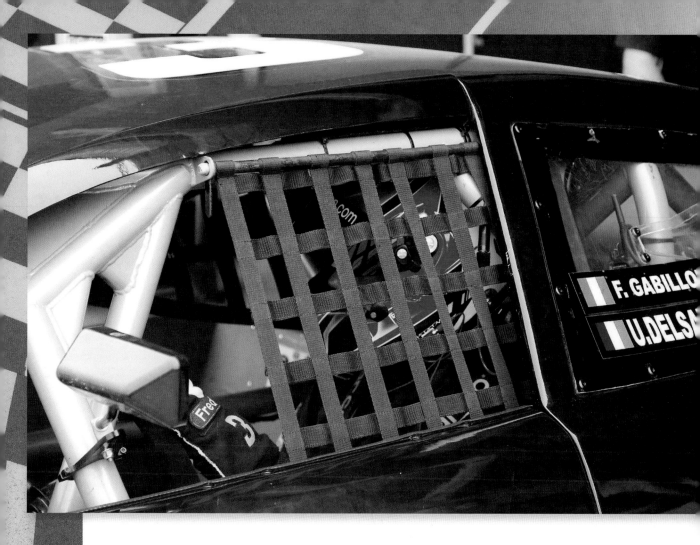

Some cars have a window net. It helps keep drivers safe. During a crash, it keeps the driver's arms inside the car.

# Race Car Diagrams

stock car

window net

slicks

spoiler

rear wing

F1 car

cockpit

slicks

front wing

## Design Your Own Race Car

If you could design your own race car, what would it look like? Would it look much like a normal car? Would the driver sit inside the car's body? Or would the car have an open cockpit? Would the tires be covered or uncovered? What color would the car's body be? Draw a picture of your race car.

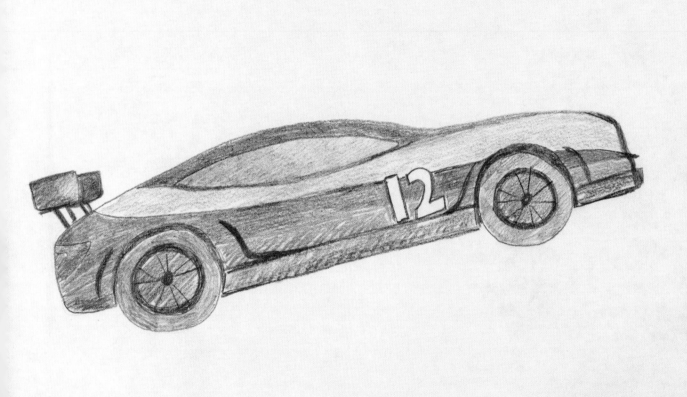

# Glossary

**cockpit** (KOK-pit)—the place where a driver sits in a race car

**decal** (DEE-kal)—a picture or label that can be put on hard surfaces

**dragster** (DRAG-stur)—a type of car built to race in a straight line against another car for a short distance on a paved track

**engine** (EN-juhn)—a machine that uses fuel to power a vehicle

**groove** (GROOV)—a long cut in something

**harness** (HAR-niss)—a set of straps used to help keep a race car driver safe

**paved** (PAYVD)—covered with a hard material such as concrete or asphalt

**spoiler** (SPOI-lur)—a winglike device attached to the back of a race car

**wing** (WING)—a long, flat panel on the front or back of some race cars

# Read More

Adamson, Thomas K. *Indy Cars*. Minneapolis: Bellwether Media, Inc., 2019.

Doeden, Matt. *Stock Cars*. North Mankato, MN: Capstone Press, a Capstone imprint, 2019.

Reinke, Beth Bence. *Race Cars on the Go*. Minneapolis: Lerner Publications, 2018.

# Internet Sites

*IndyCar Series: Anatomy of an Indy Car*
https://www.indycar.com/Fan-Info/INDYCAR-101/The-Car-Dallara/Anatomy-Of-An-INDYCAR

*NASCAR Kids*
https://www.accelerationnation.com/

*Wonderopolis: How Does an Engine Work?*
https://www.wonderopolis.org/wonder/how-does-an-engine-work

# Index

cockpits, 7, 8

crews, 8

decals, 14

engines, 10–11

Formula 1 cars, 7

harnesses, 8

IndyCars, 7

slicks, 12

spoilers, 16

steering wheels, 8

stock cars, 6

tires, 12, 16

top fuel dragsters, 10

tracks, 4, 12, 14, 16

wheels, 7

window nets, 17

wings, 16